Dogs Having Fun

(DOGS AROUND THE WORLD)

Speedy Publishing LLC
40 E. Main St. #1156
Newark, DE 19711
www.speedypublishing.com

Each dog has his own unique characteristics and personality. But one thing is certain - these loveable and delightful buddies are fascinating creatures.

A dog's shoulder blades are unattached to the rest of the skeleton to allow greater flexibility for running.

Humans can detect sounds at 20,000 times per second, while dogs can sense frequencies of 30,000 times per second.

Not all dogs are born swimmers. Some dogs need to be encouraged to swim. Some breeds are more natural swimmers than others.

Dogs have three eyelids. The third lid, called a nictitating membrane or "haw," keeps the eye lubricated and protected.

Touch is the first sense the dog develops. The entire body, including the paws, is covered with touch-sensitive nerve endings.

Dalmatian puppies are born completely white and develop their spots over time!

Dogs can see in color, though they most likely see colors similar to a color-blind human. They can see better when the light is low.

If you leave your dog a piece of clothing that smells like you, the scent will comfort them and it can help suppress their separation anxiety.

Dogs' noses secrete a thin layer of mucous that helps them absorb scent. They then lick their noses to sample the scent through their mouth.

Unlike humans, dogs typically do not need additional vitamin C. Dogs manufacture vitamin C through their glandular systems.

The most popular male dog names are Max and Jake. The most popular female dog names are Maggie and Molly.

Dogs naturally like to play keep-away better than fetch. You'll need to train your dog to play fetch, but not keep-away.

An unsupervised dog will get bored in a back yard very quickly. It is never safe to leave your dog unattended in the yard.

Dogs are about as smart as a two- or three-year-old child. This means they can understand about 150-200 words, including signals and hand movements with the same meaning as words.

www.ingramcontent.com/pod-product-compliance
Lightning Source LLC
LaVergne TN
LVHW060833170826
845678LV00010B/1969

* 9 7 9 8 8 6 9 4 5 3 4 9 5 *